ADA TWIST, SCIENTIST

THE WHY FILES

ROCKIN' ROBOTS!

By Andrea Beaty and Dr. Theanne Griffith

Amulet Books • New York

To Aaron. Welcome to the world! —A.B.

For Penny and Baby Camilla —T.G.

PUBLISHER'S NOTE: This is a work of fiction. Names, characters, places, and incidents are either the product of the author's imagination or used fictitiously, and any resemblance to actual persons, living or dead, business establishments, events, or locales is entirely coincidental.

Library of Congress Control Number 2023941540

ISBN 978-1-4197-7042-5

ADA TWIST ™ Netflix. Used with permission.
Story and text © 2024 Andrea Beaty
ADA TWIST series imagery © 2024 Netflix, Inc. and used with permission from Netflix.
Ada Twist, Scientist and the Questioneers created by Andrea Beaty and David Roberts

Book design by Charice Silverman
Illustrations by Steph Stilwell

Printed and bound in China

10 9 8 7 6 5 4 3 2 1

Amulet Books are available at special discounts when purchased in quantity for premiums and promotions as well as fundraising or educational use. Special editions can also be created to specification. For details, contact specialsales@abramsbooks.com or the address below.

Amulet Books® is a registered trademark of Harry N. Abrams, Inc.

Images courtesy Shutterstock.com: Cover: *plate of cookies*, Martin Gardeazabal; *cookie*, smikeymikey1; *yellow robot art*, Timofeev Vladimir. **Page 2** *robot dog*, Xolodan; *manager engineer check*, PopTika. **Page 3**: *quadcopter*, Alexander Piragis. **Page 4** *underwater hands-free drone*, Kryvenok Anastasiia; *vacuum robot*, Krakenimages.com. **Page 5**: *child with toy robot dog*, goodmoments. **Page 12**: *artificial robotic arm*, Mike_shots. **Page 13**: *robot with spray*, Dmytro Zinkevych; *Agriculture robotic*, Suwin. **Page 16**: *automobile production*, Jenson. **Page 17**: *engineer check*, PopTika. **Page 21**: *robot vacuum*, s.chanakanon. **Page 23**: *Honda ASIMO*, DenisKlimov. **Page 27**: *smart robotic farmers*, kung_tom. **Page 28**: *elderly care robot*, PaO_STUDIO. **Page 29**: *service robot*, Miriam Doerr Martin Frommherz. **Page 33**: *St. Petersburg*, StockphotoVideo. **Page 35**: *robot hand*, sdecoret. **Page 36**: *robot handling cookies*, Westend61 on Offset. **Pages 42, 49**: Pressmaster. **Pages 43, 50**: Stefano Mazzola. **Page 45**: *software engineer*, SeventyFour; *program source code*, BEST-BACKGROUNDS. **Page 46**: *AI chatbot*, Thapana_Studio. **Page 48**: *error message*, Besjunior. **Page 60**: *diverse school children*, Ground Picture. **Page 61**: *engineer cooperation*, WHYFRAME. **Page 65**: *agriculture robot*, Suwin. **Throughout**: *School supplies*, Green Leaf. ***Images courtesy public domain***: **Cover**: *Starships at Kingston*, StevePotter49; *glass of milk*, NIAID. **Page 1**: *delivery robot*, Sillerkiil. **Page 3**: *hexa*, Soul Train. **Page 6**: *Philon*, Eunostos. **Page 7**: *Gakutensoku*, Jin Kemoole. **Page 8**: *PUMA robot*, UL Digital Library; *Unimate pouring coffee*, Frank Q. Brown. **Page 9**: *Boss Nova scanning robot*, Saucy; *SpotMini*, David Pérez (DPC); *Parallax Activity Bot*, Elektor Labs. **Pages 14, 22**: *robots*, Steve Jurvetson. **Page 15**: *Autoproduktion*, Gilly Berlin. **Page 18**: *tiny robotic crab (all images)*, Northwestern University. **Page 19**: *UK search & rescue team*, Department for International Development/Ed Hawkesworth. **Page 20**: *BYU Mars Rover*, Peter Hyatt. **Page 21**: *Mars Spirit*, NASA. **Page 26**: *Brighton Mini Maker Fair*, Jeremy Keith. **Page 32**: *YandexRobotArizona*, Shvicha. **Page 34**: *hands and threads*, Alberto Buscató Vázquez; *robot_ABB*, Peter Potrowl. **Page 35**: *Changi Airport*, Sharon Hahn Darlin. **Page 36**: John Carkeet. **Page 41**: *motherboard*, Mbrickn. **Page 58**: *glorious rain*, Christopher Michel. **Page 61**: *NASA ISS downlink at South River High School*, NASA/Goddard/Bill Hrybyk; *PHS Robotics*, Virginia Department of Education. **Page 66**: *Ada Lovelace*, Science Museum Group. **Page 67**: *Prof. dr. Ruzena Bajcsy*, Franc Solina.

ABRAMS The Art of Books
195 Broadway, New York, NY 10007
abramsbooks.com

I saw a machine roll down the sidewalk all by itself. It delivered a package to my neighbor! Mom said it was a robot.

WHAT MAKES A ROBOT A ROBOT?

It's a mystery! A riddle!
A puzzle! A quest!

Time to find out
what robots are
about!

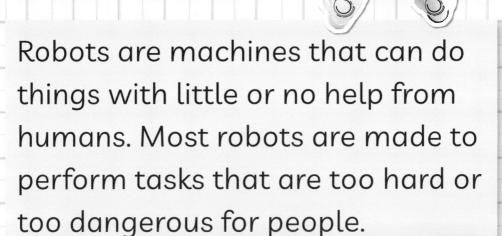

Robots are machines that can do things with little or no help from humans. Most robots are made to perform tasks that are too hard or too dangerous for people.

Some robots explore hard-to-reach places, such as the inside of a volcano or the bottom of the ocean.

Robots can also make life easier for people. Some are created to help us clean our houses or serve food in restaurants.

And some robots are made to make our lives more fun! Scientists and engineers have made robots that look and act like pets such as dogs and guinea pigs.

- Scientists have discovered statues with moving joints made about 25,000 years ago! These are the first known signs that humans were trying to create what today we call robots.

- Some of the first machines built to perform tasks for humans were made 4,000 years ago in ancient Egypt. The Egyptians built water-powered clocks!

- 2,000 years ago, ancient Greek scholars created animal- and human-like machines that appeared to move on their own. Most of these "robots" were used for entertainment.

- The first robot built in Asia was called **GAKUTENSOKU**. It was made in the late 1920s by Makoto Nishimura and used air pressure to move its head and hands.

- **UNIMATE** was the name of the first computer-controlled robot. Unimate was invented by George Devol in 1954.

Robot Hall of Famer!

Robots are not just machines that act and look like humans. In fact, most robots don't look like humans at all!

What a robot does and what it looks like depends on why that robot was made in the first place. Not all robots have the exact same parts. But there are a few important things to think about when building a robot.

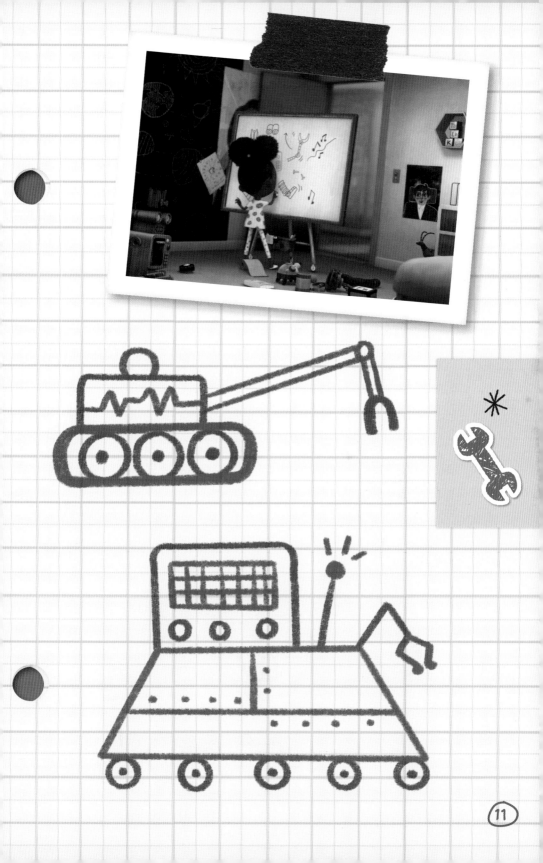

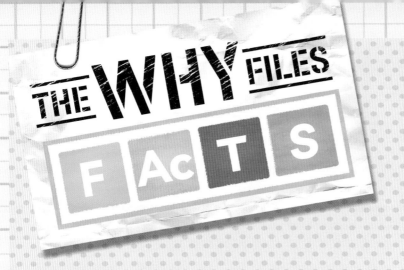

ROBOT BUILDING BLOCKS

- A robot's **SIZE**, **SHAPE**, and **WEIGHT** will determine what kind of tasks it can do.

- All robots **MOVE** to perform their jobs, and some robots need good **FINE MOTOR SKILLS** to do more complicated tasks.

- Robots must be able to **SENSE** the environment around them.

- Robots need **ENERGY** to do their jobs.

- Robots must be able to **FOLLOW INSTRUCTIONS**.

Robots come in all different **sizes** and **shapes**. Most robots used in factories are big. That is because they need to be able to lift and carry heavy things.

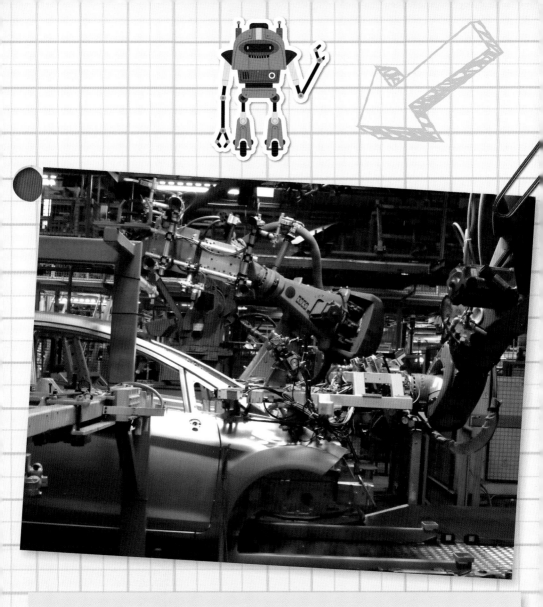

Robots used in factories also **weigh** a lot themselves. If they were too light, they could fall over or break!

Factory robots are often shaped like human arms and hands. That's because they do tasks that humans do with their arms and hands! These robots are called **robotic arms**.

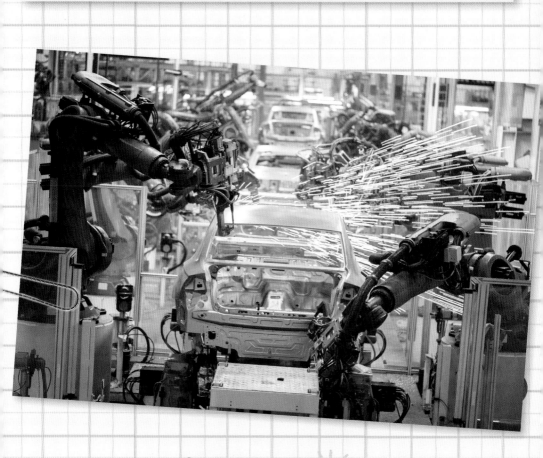

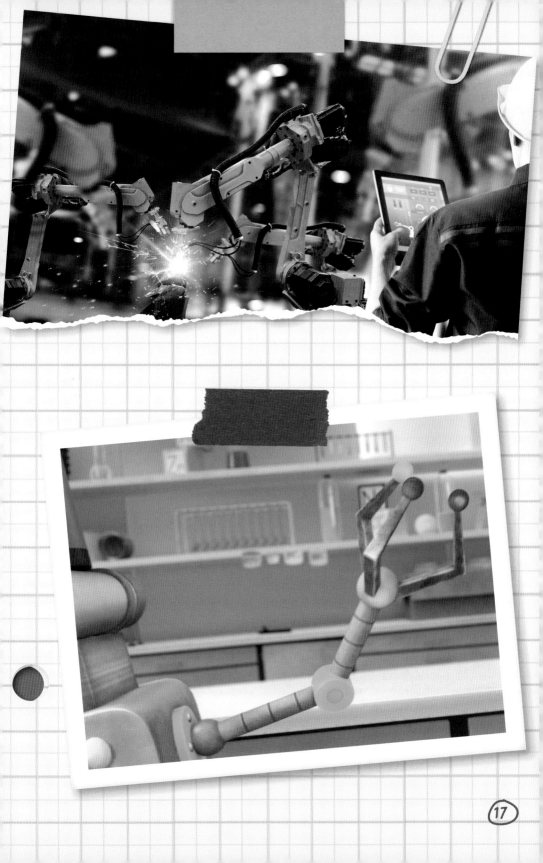

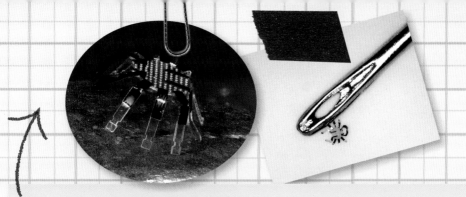

Some robots are small. Scientists are working hard to create tiny robots called **microbots**. Microbots are smaller than one square millimeter. That's about five times smaller than a grain of rice! Because of their small size, microbots could be used in large numbers called swarms.

For example, thousands of microbots could be released at the site of a natural disaster, like an earthquake or a tornado. They would help find people trapped under fallen buildings.

Robots are made to **move**. Some move from a fixed spot, like the robotic arm. But other kinds of robots can travel.

Some use wheels that are controlled by a motor, such as the robots that explore Mars. Robots that are used to vacuum floors also use wheels.

"Legged robots" are built with legs that look more like human, animal, or insect legs. These robots can have eight legs or more and can go places that robots with wheels cannot. For example, legged robots can climb stairs. Robots that only have wheels cannot.

23

But some robots are made with both legs and wheels. The wheels help the robot move fast, and the legs allow the robot to do more complex movements. Robots with legs on wheels may be the way of the future!

Fine motor skills are used to make small but difficult movements. Buttoning a shirt, writing neatly, using scissors, drawing a picture, and tying shoelaces are all examples of using the fine motor skills that children learn as they grow.

For robots to do some of the complex jobs that humans perform, they also need to have good fine motor skills. For example, robots that work on farms must be able to grip delicate fruits and vegetables carefully without smashing them.

In the future, robots can help people who have trouble moving perform daily tasks such as getting dressed and brushing teeth. These robots will need very good fine motor skills!

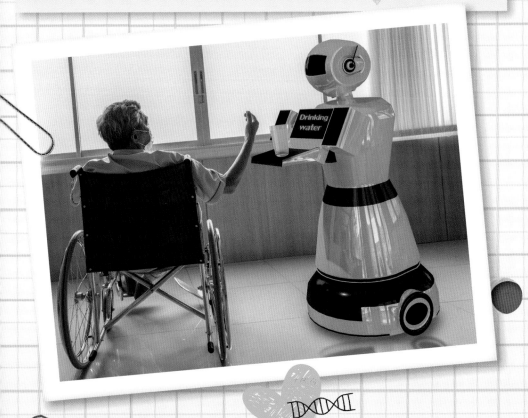

Awesome possum! Robots can help people do all kinds of things!

ROBOT!

(a poem by Ada Twist)

If I had a robot,

I'd have it make ten more.

If each of them would do
the same,

I'd start a robot store!

I SEE ROBOTS, BUT CAN THEY SEE ME?

Just like us, robots need to **sense** the world around them. Robots use devices called **sensors** that give them important information about the environment they are in and the objects they are using.

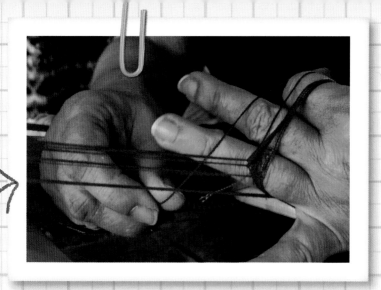

The skin of our hands allows us to feel the shape and size of an object as well as its texture and temperature. Instead of skin, robots use touch sensors to feel.

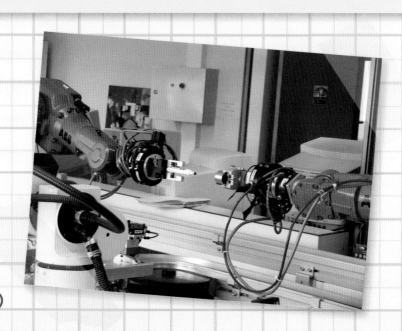

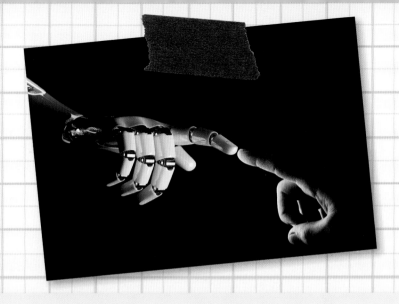

Instead of eyes, robots use cameras or light sensors to see.

Robots can also use smell and sound sensors to figure out what and where things are.

Robots used in the food industry are even learning how to taste with special taste sensors! This could become very important for testing food safety.

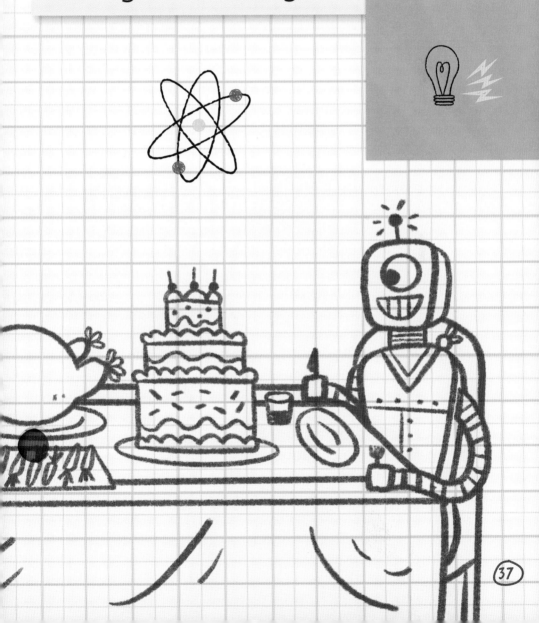

We need **energy** in order to do things—and so do robots!

We get our energy from the food we eat. Robots do not eat food. Most robots get their energy from electricity. This electricity could come from batteries, or the source could even be solar energy from the sun.

One of the most important things all robots must do is to **follow instructions**.

We use our brains to follow instructions. Robots do not have brains like ours. A robot has a minicomputer inside it that acts like a brain and tells the robot what to do.

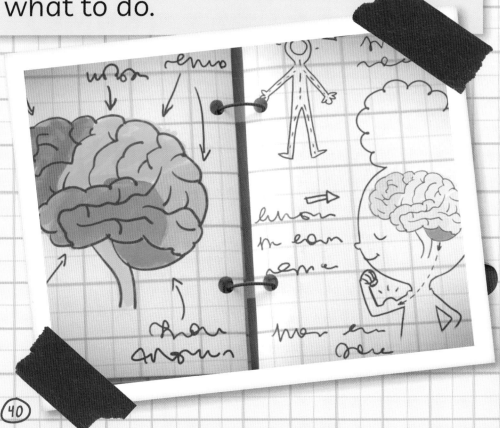

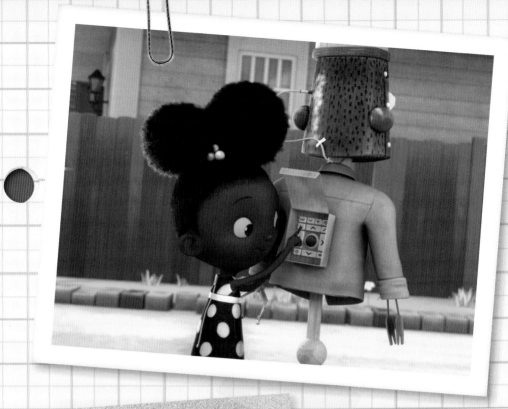

micro-computer from inside a robot

Sometimes people think robots and computers are the same. But robots and computers are quite different.

Robots are machines that are built to move and perform jobs. Computers are devices that use math and codes to handle and store large amounts of information.

π

$E=mc^2$

For example, robots found in some restaurants can deliver food to customers. A computer cannot do that! A computer can only store information about how many orders were placed and what people ate.

FEATURES	ROBOTS	COMPUTERS
Move	Yes	No
Handle and store information	No	Yes
Sense the environment	Yes	No
Follow Instructions	Yes!	Yes!

I read books and learn things from other people.

HOW DO ROBOTS LEARN WHAT TO DO?

People use written languages to give instructions to the minicomputers inside robots. Those languages are called **codes**, and writing the language is called **coding** or **programming**.

lines of code!

People who write code are called **coders** or **programmers**. Each type of code uses a different set of letters or order of words to communicate. Just as humans speak different languages, so do robots!

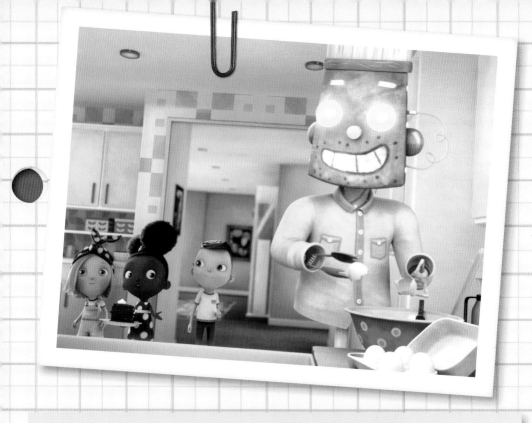

Coding is like creating a recipe. Recipes tell you more than just which ingredients you need. They also tell you how much of each ingredient to add, when and how to add the ingredients, and how long each step in the recipe should take.

Programmers must put this type of information into their codes, too. If a code is not clear, a robot will not understand what its minicomputer is trying to communicate. The robot could end up performing the wrong task or be unable to stop doing a task.

I think I've connected the polka dots! Robots can do lots of things for us, but first, we have to tell them what to do. And how to do it!

There are a few common ways that coders give instructions to robots.

THE WHY FILES
F AcT S

WAYS TO CODE A ROBOT

- LOOPING
- SEQUENCING
- BRANCHING
- SELECTION

A **loop** is a set of instructions that repeats over and over in the same order. Your bedtime routine is like a loop. Every night, you take a bath, change into pajamas, brush your teeth, read a bedtime story, and turn off the lights.

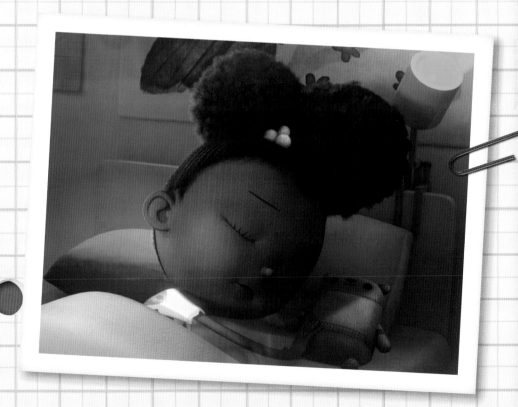

In the future, a robot might help you with bedtime! It would be important to write a clear loop for your bedtime code.

Otherwise, the robot might turn off the lights before you brush your teeth!

It is also important to stop a loop at the right time. A bedtime robot needs to know that after the lights are turned off, the loop is complete until the next night. If not, your bedtime routine would never end!

A **sequence** is the order of steps in a code. It is important to know which step to do first, second, third . . . until the end of the code.

Coders use **branching** or **selection** to help robots make choices using a set of rules.

For example, if the rule is that bedtime starts at 7:00 p.m. on weekdays but 8:30 p.m. on weekends, you could tell a robot helper to follow this set of instructions by creating a "weekend branch" in your bedtime code. It would tell the robot: "On weekends, start bedtime routine at 8:30 p.m."

Yay!

BRANCHING

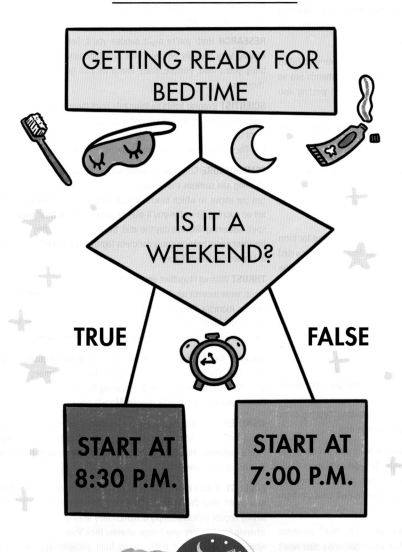

GETTING READY FOR BEDTIME

IS IT A WEEKEND?

TRUE

FALSE

START AT 8:30 P.M.

START AT 7:00 P.M.

Coders also use "if-then" selection statements to help robots to make choices. **If** it is raining, **then** you need an umbrella. **If** it is hot and sunny, **then** you need to put on sunscreen. You could use if-then selection statements to create a code that tells a robot that **if** it is raining, **then** pack an umbrella.

SELECTION

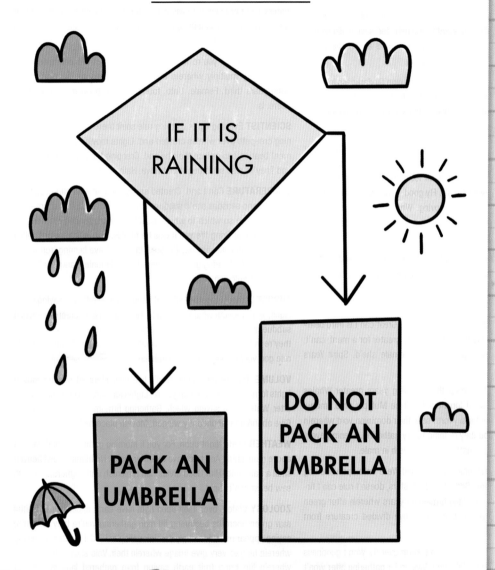

IF IT IS RAINING

PACK AN UMBRELLA

DO NOT PACK AN UMBRELLA

The study of robots is called **robotics**. Robotic scientists create new and better robots and help create code for the robots to follow. They also study ways to make robots cost less to build so that more people can use them.

I have an idea! If I work very hard, I can build a robot to do my work so I won't have to work so hard!

WE NEED A BRAINSTORM

I'm helping Dad in the garden. Could robots help, too?

Robots could drill holes to plant flower seeds.

And test the soil and add water when it's too dry.

They could measure the plants and harvest the tomatoes when they are ripe.

Robots could keep away pests like slugs . . . and my brother!

ADA LOVELACE

(1815–1852) was born before computers and robots were invented, but she wrote the first-ever code for a machine. The first modern code was named after her and called ADA.

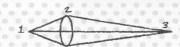

RUZENA BAJCSY (b. 1933) is one of the first modern female robotic scientists. Her research helped figure out new ways to make robot vision sensors better.

AYANNA HOWARD (b. 1972) is the first woman to lead the Ohio State University College of Engineering. She studies the best ways that humans and robots can interact with one another.

SILAS ADEKUNLE (b. 1991) is a Nigerian inventor who created the first intelligent gaming robot, called MekaMon. Through a Bluetooth connection to a smart device, MekaMon can play virtual games in the real world! MekaMon can even learn and gets better the more it plays.

I have MORE QUESTIONS now than I did before.

Why does each question lead to three questions more?

Is answering that what science is for?

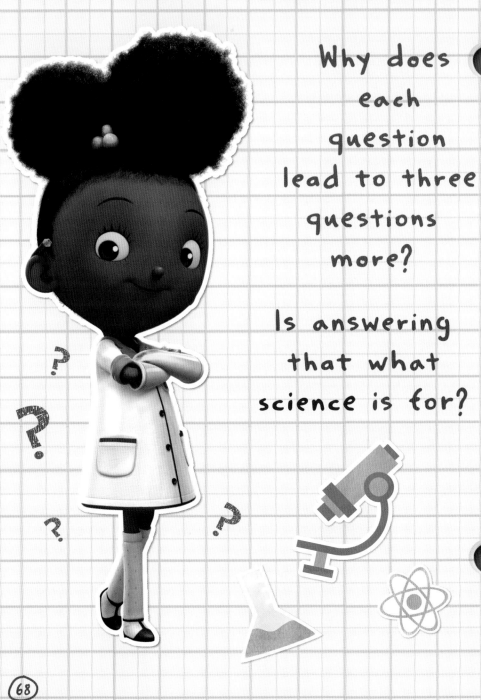

MY QUESTIONS!

Do robots have feelings?

Can they make smells?

Can robots grow?

Do robots have names?

If people build robots to make things, can robots build robots, too?

Can robots teach themselves new things?

Are robots intelligent?

What is artificial intelligence?
Are robots funny?

Do robots have families?

Are there robots in space?

Can robots exist inside people?

SIMPLE
SCIENCE
EXPERIMENTS

You can ask a grown-up for help!

BUILD A ROBOTIC ARM!

MATERIALS

- Hole punch

- 2 large paper clips

- Marker

- 1 medium brass fastener (about 1 inch long)

- 1 paper cup

- 2 feet of smooth string, like fishing line or kite string

- 1 straw

- Corrugated cardboard (the kind that has grooves in the middle—most shipping boxes use corrugated cardboard)

- Tape

INSTRUCTIONS

1. Cut one 2-x-4-inch and one 2-x-8-inch strip of cardboard. Punch a hole in one corner of each strip. The longer strip is the "arm," and the shorter strip is the "hand."

2 Cut the straw into 1-inch-long pieces.

3 Unbend one paper clip to make a hook shape, and tape it to the inside of the cup.

4 Line up the holes in each strip of cardboard, and connect them using the brass fastener. Do not make the fastener too tight or your arm won't be able to move.

5 Tape about 3–4 pieces of straw down the middle of the large cardboard strip, and tape 2–3 pieces down the middle of the smaller strip.

6 Thread the string through the straw guides, and tape the string end to the hand section. Pull the string to make sure the arm moves. If it doesn't, the brass fastener may be too tight.

7 Unbend the second paper clip to make a hook, and pull the straight end into a groove in the cardboard at the end of the hand.

8 Use tape to fix the hook in place.

9 Time to test! Place the paper cup on the table, and bring the robotic arm toward it. Try to hook the cup and lift!

Share your results on social media using #whyfileswonders!

BUILD YOUR OWN ROBOT!

MATERIALS

- Empty plastic bottle
- Aluminum foil
- Knife
- Pipe cleaners*
- 3 pencils
- Glue

- Tape
- Googly eyes*
- Sequins, rhinestones, stickers*
- Black permanent marker
- 2 bottle caps

*These items are optional! You can use them or something else to decorate your robot!

INSTRUCTIONS

1. Glue foil strips onto the plastic bottle, making sure it is covered entirely in foil.

2 Use scissors to create small holes in the side of the plastic bottle. They should be just big enough to fit a pencil snugly.

3 Make the arms by wrapping a pipe cleaner around each pencil. If you don't have pipe cleaners, think of another fun way to decorate your robot arms!

4 Stick the pencils into each little hole on the side of the plastic bottle.

5 Use your scissors again to poke small holes in the bottle caps. Stick the pencil through the holes. The bottle caps should be at each end of the pencil.

6 Tape a pencil to the bottom of your robot.

7 Time to get creative! Decorate your robot! You can use googly eyes, or draw eyes on. You can add stickers. It's up to you!

Share your robots on social media using #whyfileswonders!

Andrea Beaty

is the bestselling author of the Questioneers series and many other books. She has a degree in biology and computer science. Andrea lives outside Chicago where she writes books for kids and plants flowers for birds, bees, and bugs. Learn more about her books at AndreaBeaty.com.

Sirk Productions

Theanne Griffith, PhD,

is a brain scientist by day and a storyteller by night. She is the lead investigator of a neuroscience laboratory at the University of California–Davis and author of the science adventure series The Magnificent Makers. She lives in Northern California with her family. Learn more about her STEM-themed books at TheanneGriffith.com.

Samantha Jovan Photography

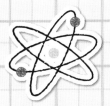

CHECK OUT THESE OTHER BOOKS STARRING
ADA TWIST, SCIENTIST

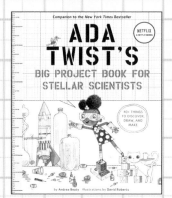

There's more to discover at **Questioneers.com**.